Pathfinder 37

Differentiation and individual learners:
a guide for classroom practice

The *Pathfinder* Series

All Pathfinders are available through good book suppliers or direct from **Grantham Book Services**, Isaac Newton Way, Alma Park Industrial Estate, Grantham, Lincs NG31 9SD. Fax orders to: 01476 541 061. Credit card orders: 01476 541 080.

Pathfinder 37

A CILT series for language teachers

Differentiation and individual learners

A guide for classroom practice

Anne Convery and Do Coyle

Centre for Information
on Language Teaching and Research

First published 1999
Copyright © 1999 Centre for Information on Language Teaching and Research
ISBN 1 902031 10 5

A catalogue record of this book is available from the British Library
Printed in Great Britain by Copyprint UK Ltd

Published by the Centre for Information on Language Teaching and Research,
20 Bedfordbury, Covent Garden, London WC2N 4LB
Typesetting by Karin Erskine, Croydon

CILT publications are available from Grantham Book Services, Isaac Newton Way, Alma Park
Industrial Estate, Grantham, Lincs NG31 8SD. Tel: 01476 541 080. Fax: 01476 541 061.
Book trade representation (UK and Ireland): Broadcast Book Services, 24 De Montfort Road,
London SW16 1LZ. Tel: 0181 677 5129.

Contents

Foreword

It is now five years since the publication of Pathfinder 18, *Differentiation — taking the initiative*. The original book represented a collection of ideas on differentiation for developing classroom practice.

Having visited many schools in the ensuing period, it has been both stimulating and encouraging to evaluate current practice with regard to differentiation, since so much has now become part of general departmental policy and integrated into teaching repertoires.

Following the professional development cycle, the time is now right to re-examine the principles of differentiation in the light of current educational thinking and to look forward to refining and enhancing classroom practice over the next five years. The philosophy of this new edition reflects the general move away from a teacher-centred approach to differentiation to one which focuses more closely on individual learners.

We should like to thank colleagues in our Partnership schools and here in the School of Education at the University of Nottingham for sharing their ideas and offering practical assistance. Thanks also to our student teachers who never fail to challenge and question our thinking and whose enthusiasm for becoming successful teachers has played such an important role in encouraging a realistic yet creative approach to differentiated learning.

Anne Convery
Do Coyle

Introduction: How are learners different?

INDIVIDUALS

Any group of learners, whether it be a set, a stream, a band or a mixed ability class, is made up of a number of very different individuals. As teachers, our job is to get to know these individuals very well in order to be able to match work as closely as possible to their needs and abilities.

All too often discussion of differentiation can become focused on the notion of ability, or achievement, and that can prevent us from looking further. However, there are many other differences between young learners, and an appreciation of them can really help to enhance our understanding of differentiation and to shift the emphasis away from the notion of ability.

INDIVIDUAL DIFFERENCES

Whilst working with trainee teachers over a number of years we have always encouraged them to start thinking about differentiation by considering as many factors as they can which make children different from one another. The trainees are asked to record their ideas on pieces of coloured card, which are then stuck onto a white board at the front of the room (see Figure 1 overleaf).

This visual display makes a powerful impact on the trainees and leads us into a discussion about how learners are different from one another. Although schools may often choose organisational structures which group individual students together for learning according to ability or achievement, this activity brings out a whole range of other factors which can influence the way young learners may work in the classroom.

It can be helpful to divide these factors into three groups: social, affective and intellectual (see Figure 2). Whilst these factors are common to us all, what makes each individual unique is the complete interplay between the three. As teachers, it is important to be aware of our students as individuals, and to tailor our teaching, as fas as possible, to their wants and needs.

THE CHILD

culture & background

age, maturity

gender

motivation

prior knowledge

ability

attention span

outside interests

speed of work

relationships

parental support

Figure 1

c*i*LT

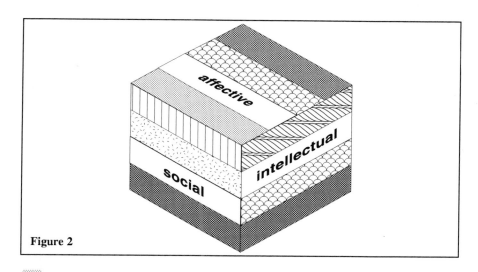

Figure 2

DIFFERENT STRATEGIES

Following on from the awareness-raising activity, we ask our trainee teachers to try and identify strategies for coping with the differences that have been highlighted, for example, if they noticed that a particular gender group was dominant in a class, what would they do about it? At this stage, the strategies discussed are general and not subject-specific. Some examples are found in the box below, and others are listed in the Appendix. It is important to begin a book on differentiation by looking closely at the individuals who make up our classes. Building relationships takes time, and therefore matching work to individuals' needs and abilities gets easier as the teacher's relationship with the class grows stronger. It is also vital to obtain as much additional information as possible about each individual, gradually piecing it together, as in a huge jigsaw puzzle.

Individual differences	Suggested strategies
Gender	• experiment with seating arrangements • direct questions equally to boys and girls • organise activities that oblige students to mix naturally e.g. surveys
Outside interests	• find ways of allowing students to share their interests in class • talk to students informally about their interests
Parental support	• allow students to do their homework at school, if they wish

CiLT

Having started from the premise that each learner is an individual, it clearly follows that learning is an individual process. Each person has their own particular learning needs and styles. Each learner has their own learning preference, for example, there are learners who genuinely do not wish to speak out in class, but prefer to reflect 'privately' upon classroom events.

By contrast, however, most teaching in schools is organised in larger groups of learners and it is the teacher's job to provide an effective learning environment. Teachers faced with this anomaly have to make conscious critical choices about how to organise the task of teaching the individuals within learning groups. These choices are critical since they may help or hinder learning. The effectiveness of teaching depends on its impact on learning – that is when it provides the most accessible learning opportunities for the widest range of learners. In other words, the teacher is responsible for accommodating a range of **learning styles** by varying his or her own **teaching style**. Identifying and understanding teaching and learning styles is therefore essential in establishing a basis from which to create a differentiated learning environment. It is only relatively recently that this issue has received serious attention as an important factor in organising effective modern foreign language classrooms. We shall return to this issue in chapter 6.

DEFINITIONS

It is important to clarify at an early stage what we mean and understand by the term 'differentiation'. The relevant literature provides several acceptable definitions, including our own from Pathfinder 18, which help to shed light on different aspects of this complex issue.

Differentiation is...

> '... the process by which teachers provide opportunities for pupils to achieve their potential, working at their own pace through a variety of relevant learning activities.' (Convery and Coyle, 1993)

> '... the process by which curriculum objectives, teaching methods, assessment methods, resources and learning activities are planned to cater for the needs of individual students.' (*Science and Pupils with SEN*, NCC, 1991)

> '... the process which goes on in classrooms which enables pupils to achieve their maximum potential. It is about meeting the educational needs of all pupils and giving them access to their curriculum entitlement.' (Visser, 1993)

C*i*LT

The concept of differentiation is open to wide interpretation. The National Curriculum formalised the notion of the entitlement of every learner to have his or her individual needs catered for.

> *'Whether pupils are taught in sets or mixed-ability groups, there will be a range of attainment and interests. The presence of bilingual pupils and pupils with SEN further widens the range of language attainment in a class. Differentiation is essential if all pupils are to have the opportunities to achieve their full potential. Differentiation is linked to progression.'*
>
> (*MFL Non-Statutory Guidance*, NCC, 1992)

It thus becomes the responsibility of every teacher to find effective ways of dealing with these needs, and although the challenges of differentiation might appear in some ways daunting, the ideas contained in this Pathfinder work on the principle of 'starting small'. Differentiation does not necessarily mean abandoning existing materials but rather building on current practice – to involve teachers in making decisions regarding **core work** (generally regarded as suitable for **all** students) and **branching work** – which will take account of individual goals, interests and needs. After all:

> *'The setting of different tasks to different pupils does not have to take place all the time.'*
>
> (Wringe, 1989)

In Chapter 1 we shall look at different ways of differentiating.

1   Ways of differentiating: matching learners and activities

Different authors have identified different ways of differentiating and to a certain extent, we feel that it does not matter a great deal which type of differentiation is being used, as long as an attempt is being made by the teacher to match learners and activities. However, it is helpful at this stage to examine more closely some of the ways in which teachers can organise differentiated learning (see Figure 3).

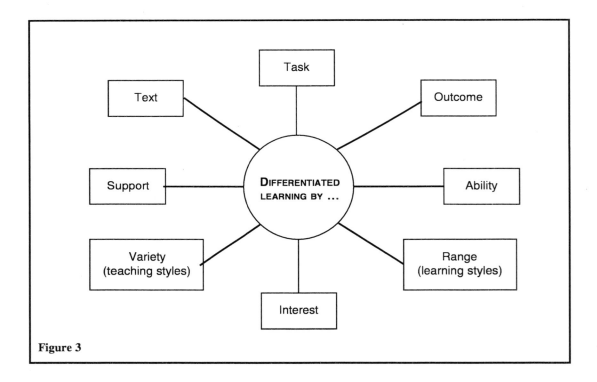

Figure 3

There is in practice a good deal of overlap between the types identified in Figure 3, and any one activity may involve two, three, four or more of the above at the same time. It may be useful at this point to examine each category more closely:

C*i*LT

By text

Learners work with spoken or written materials (referred to as text in the National Curriculum and other sources) at different levels of difficulty on the same subject or topic area. The teacher thus ensures that all learners cover the same ground, whilst at the same time matching different levels of complexity to students' differing needs. For example, an authentic recording of a weather forecast may be appropriate for the most able learners in a group, whereas a commercially-produced cassette recording of an 'imaginary' weather forecast may be more suited to other learners in the group. Similarly, an article from an authentic newspaper or magazine could be used by more able learners, whilst other learners use an article from a coursebook, which could be further adapted by the teacher to support the weaker learners if necessary. An appropriate text can always be written or recorded by the teacher and/or Foreign Language Assistant if one cannot be found in existing resources.

By task

Learners may be working on the same text, but the tasks they are required to do can be graded in difficulty and matched to differing needs and abilities. For example, when all learners in a group are working on a reading activity, the less able learners can be supported by tasks which do not require them to understand every word, but rather the gist of what they read. The more able learners can be asked more searching questions. Similarly, when engaged in a listening activity, the less able learners may be required to identify only a minimum amount of information, whereas more able learners could be set a more open-ended task.

By outcome

Learners are all engaged in the same task but produce widely differing end results. For example, when working on a differentiated worksheet, some students may complete one or two of the tasks, ticking boxes or completing gap-filling exercises, whereas other students may work quickly through the initial tasks and tackle the more open-ended tasks at the end. Alternatively, when learners are required to write a letter to a pen-friend the teacher can expect results ranging from a few lines of factual information through to a more substantial piece of a descriptive and imaginative nature. What is of crucial importance when differentiating by outcome is that the teacher has decided in advance what the expected outcomes will be, and that these are communicated to the learners. For example, a Year 10 class had to write as a homework task a paragraph of about 150 words on what they were like as a child, following these assessment criteria:

<table>
<tr>
<td>

ALL of you must . . .

- incorporate at least 5 of the new vocabulary items studied this week
- use the imperfect tense correctly
- use the model provided to help you

</td>
<td>

SOME of you might . . .

- be creative and humorous
- extend and develop the model provided

</td>
</tr>
</table>

It is important that all learners feel that their work is valued by the teacher, for example, that they all have an opportunity to display their work in the classroom. In this respect, the use of IT can help in terms of presentation, for however simple or complex the piece of work, all work being displayed can look neat and be legible if it has been word-processed.

BY SUPPORT

The teacher can ensure that differentiation takes place by the amount of additional support offered to learners of all abilities in terms of time, resources and tasks. This may involve the presence of a support or a special needs teacher or Foreign Language Assistant who works alongside specific groups of students during the lesson. In some schools, sixth-form foreign language students offer additional help in lower school lessons. Alternatively, whilst learners are working in groups or individually, the teacher is freed to work with a small group (reinforcing a point already covered, for example) or with any individual learner who needs further help or encouragement.

However, support does not necessarily have to be in the form of extra teachers or helpers in the room, as in many cases this would not be achievable. Differentiation by support can be provided in a variety of ways, involving resources and tasks. For example, if students are working independently on a task with instructions in the target language, a support card can be prepared by the teacher to which students can refer without having to go directly to the teacher. The card might be in the form of a checklist, containing symbols or English, when appropriate. Other forms of support include wall displays, posters, mobiles and personal cassettes with common classroom instructions, useful phrases, new vocabulary, numbers and so on, as an ever-present reminder to which students can refer if and when necessary.

BY ABILITY

Learners are grouped by ability for teaching and learning purposes. This could be across a year group (setting) or within one class. Work is then organised to match the ability and needs of each class/group. There is some overlap here with differentiation by text. This arrangement may be of use if the teacher wishes a particular group of learners to study something which would not be appropriate for all the learners (a more complex point of grammar, for example, or the reinforcement of a point covered in an earlier lesson).

BY INTEREST

Learners are allowed to pursue something which interests them personally, and are given a degree of choice, or 'guided choice' in selecting activities. This could involve choice in the use of equipment (listening station, video, Language Master, computer, Concept Keyboard), choice in the skill involved (listening, speaking, reading, writing), choice in the task or choice in the topic or subject matter. Learners who are given the opportunity to study something they are really interested in will be more highly motivated, and hopefully this will have a knock-on effect in other areas of their work. If the teacher organises a selection of activities for a particular lesson, and stipulates the minimum number to be completed by each individual by the end of the lesson, learners can then work at their own pace on their selected tasks. More able learners will complete more tasks, and may be motivated by the freedom of choice to complete all the tasks.

BY VARIETY (FOCUS ON TEACHING STYLES)

All teachers are different. They will have preferred teaching styles. However, the teacher's own awareness of 'self as learner' with preferred learning styles, is a powerful introduction to understanding the importance of motivating learners by providing them with a 'varied diet'. Extending one's teaching repertoire is an important factor in providing a stimulating learning environment.

BY RANGE (FOCUS ON LEARNING STYLES)

All learners are different. They too will have preferred learning styles. Whilst some may enjoy listening activities but feel uncomfortable speaking aloud in the target language, others may like 'having a voice' and participate willingly in paired role plays and so on. In appealing to learners' preferred styles it is a case of not being able to please all students all of the time! Instead, providing a variety of approaches and activities will ensure that equally a variety of preferences is catered for over a period of time.

Having examined the various ways of differentiating, the following chapter will provide some strategies for getting started, with reference to simple examples for immediate use in the classroom.

2   Getting started

Introducing differentiation into the teaching and learning of a foreign language need not be a daunting task. In the first instance, it does not necessarily involve the teacher in the production of masses of new materials, or in a radical change in teaching style. Indeed, many teachers who have not previously considered the concept of differentiation may find on closer examination of their teaching styles that they have been instinctively using differentiation without acknowledging it.

In this chapter, we aim to look at ways in which teachers can begin to organise differentiated learning in the classroom in a straightforward way, involving little or no additional work in terms of preparation. The ideas and suggestions which follow can be put into immediate practice.

PRESENTING NEW MATERIAL

Since individual learners have their own preferred learning style, by varying the way in which new material is presented, the teacher is providing opportunities for learners to respond in different ways. Figure 4 shows a range of possible ways in which new material can be presented.

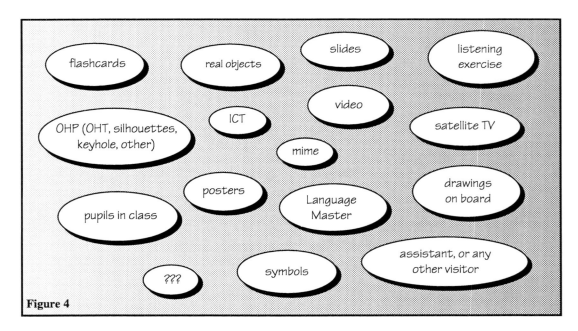

Figure 4

QUESTION AND ANSWER

As many lessons begin in this way, it is simple for the teacher to operate a differentiated form of questioning, and allow students to respond to questions at an appropriate level. Thus, at the basic level, a learner who responds with either a nod or shake of the head is demonstrating that he or she has understood the question. At the other end of the spectrum, open-ended questions will extend the most able learners. A teacher who is a skilful questioner will be able to mix up question types and carefully direct them to students in an appropriate manner. The following table contains some suggested questions, possible responses and comments on their type and usage:

QUESTION	POSSIBLE RESPONSES	COMMENTS
Tu aimes le fromage?	Nod/shake of head *Oui/Non.* *Oui, j'aime le fromage.* *Non, je n'aime pas le fromage.*	Non verbal response possible. Minimum manipulation required. Repetition of words supplied in question.
Tu préfères le fromage ou le jambon?	*Le fromage/le jambon.* *Je préfère le fromage.* *Je préfère le jambon.*	One/two word answer possible. Pupils have to choose answer from two possibilities given in question. Very little manipulation.
Tu manges du pain le matin?	*Non/Oui.* *Je mange du pain le matin.* *Je mange du pain à midi.*	One-word answer acceptable. Longer utterances using repetition or new information can be encouraged.
Qu'est-ce que tu manges le matin?	*Je mange des céréales ...*	A more open type of question but possible answers are restricted. Learners can begin to personalise their replies.
Qu'est-ce que tu aimes manger?	*J'aime les champignons, les hamburgers, le curry et la glace à la fraise.*	Open-ended question – pupils could offer one or many items in response, depending on their personal preference and based on reality.
Qu'est-ce que tu choisirais dans un restaurant français? (en regardant le menu)	*J'aimerais goûter ...* *... le cassoulet.* *... la choucroute.* *... le magret de canard.*	Open-ended question encouraging imaginative and creative responses.
Pourquoi?	*Parce que ...*	Extension or follow-up questions can challenge individuals to move their learning forwards.

Skilful handling of differentiated questioning depends largely on the teacher's knowledge of individual learners and their needs, and on his or her relationship with the learners. If these two criteria are established, the teacher can direct the questions effectively, allowing the more confident students to model answers first before requiring less confident learners to answer by reproducing an answer already heard. To help learners answer questions:

- use question types randomly, so that there is no obvious move from 'easy' to more demanding questions;
- be generous and fair in use of praise and encouragement, so that learners will realise that all responses are valued by the teacher;
- handle mistakes and wrong answers sensitively in order to create a climate in which learners can, and want to, operate according to their differing needs;
- extension idea! Be ready to help learners extend and follow-up their answers by the use of prompts, such as *pourquoi?, continue, par exemple, et puis … ?*

PAIR AND GROUP WORK

Differentiation can be achieved by organising learners to work with partners of the same, or similar, ability as themselves. Whatever the task set, or stimulus given, if a time limit is set by the teacher, or if a check is made to find out where learners are in the exercise, then pupils can work at their own pace. Able students will cover more ground and may complete the whole task in the allotted time, whereas less able students will not be under pressure to keep up with their peers.

On the other hand, less able learners also need opportunities to complete set tasks, with resulting 'job satisfaction', so it is important to vary the ways in which pair work is organised. If no time limit is set, then certain students will need extending once they have covered the main, or core, task. This can be done in a variety of ways by:

- exchanging roles;
- encouraging learners to make up their own examples;
- students of differing abilities take different roles, with the selection of roles according to different criteria (length, difficulty, importance etc);
- introducing problem-solving elements ('tell your partner that you don't have what he or she has just asked for');
- encouraging unpredictability – students can differentiate themselves and this helps them to cope with the unexpected.

C*i*LT

Almost any listening exercise which is provided on a cassette accompanying a commercial course can be differentiated by the teacher, if it has not already been done by the author. Two simple ways are:

ADDING SUPPLEMENTARY INFORMATION

Learners listen for additional information (such as other words, new expressions, interesting points) once the set exercise has been completed. This type of activity can be carried out as a whole-class activity using one cassette recorder and is not dependent, therefore, on the acquisition of more sophisticated equipment.

USING A GRID TO RECORD INFORMATION

Students are asked to add information to one column at a time, during successive listenings to the extract.

For example, with reference to the topic of train travel, many course cassettes (in any language) contain recordings of station announcements (destinations of trains, departure times, platform numbers and so on), which can be adapted to make a differentiated task. Thus a simple worksheet could be devised in any language as follows:

	A DESTINATION	B DEPARTURE TIME	C PLATFORM	D ADDITIONAL INFORMATION
1				
2				
3				
4				
5				

Column A could be the core material which all students should attempt to complete, with the subsequent columns to be filled according to the learners' strengths. The final column might only be attempted by certain learners in the class, and is designed to be open-ended.

The above table could even be written up on a board, or on an overhead transparency, one column at a time, each time the tape is replayed, with students moving on to the next column when they feel ready. Alternatively, this type of task could be developed into a jigsaw listening activity, so that each column of information could be completed by a certain group of learners, pre-selected by the teacher. Some students could complete column A, and so on, with others being expected to complete column D. When the grid part of the task has been completed, learners could be divided into groups of four, each group containing an A, B, C and D listener. The activity could then develop into an information gap oral exercise as students have to swap information in order to complete the whole grid.

READING SKILLS

Two simple ways of differentiating a written text are:

- modify the text;
- modify the task.

This means that reading tasks from coursebooks can be used with the minimum amount of extra work required to make them accessible to a greater range of pupils. In the following example, from *Zickzack Neu* Book 1 (Nelson), pupils are required to read two handwritten letters in German and to answer questions on them. It is not immediately clear to which letter the questions refer, so pupils have to search both letters for the correct answers.

Lies die Briefe und beantworte die Fragen:

Freiburg, den 22. Februar

Hallo Derek!

Du lernst Deutsch in der Schule! Toll! Wann kommst Du nach Deutschland? Du kannst zu uns kommen. Wir haben eine Wohnung in der Stadtmitte. Die Wohnung ist groß, und ich habe mein eigenes Zimmer. Du kannst mein Bett haben, und ich schlafe auf der Couch! Wann kommst du? Ich hoffe bald.

Herzliche Grüße,
Dein Werner

Appen, den 2. Januar

Liebe Linda!

Du lernst jetzt Deutsch? Klasse! Kannst Du Ende April nach Appen kommen? Das Wetter ist normalerweise gut zu Ostern. Wir haben ein Haus in Appen. Das ist ein Dorf in Norddeutschland. Das Haus steht am Marktplatz. Es ist sehr groß und alt. Wir haben eine Küche, ein Eßzimmer ein Wohnzimmer, und vier Schlafzimmer. Ich habe mein eigenes Zimmer. Es hat ein Bett und eine Couch. Du kannst das Bett haben! Meine Katze Mitzi schläft in der Ecke. Hoffentlich kommst Du Ende April!

Herzliche Grüße,
Deine Bettina

CiLT

An exercise such as this might be suitable for many students, but it may need to be modified in order to be accessible to all learners in a mixed-ability class. In the example below, the two texts have been word-processed, in order to remove any difficulty learners might have in understanding authentic handwriting. The modified task set consists of a grid, which requires students to put a tick or a cross as appropriate. The information asked for is the same for both texts. When this example was used with a class, the students could choose, with the teacher's guidance, whether they wanted to tackle the textbook or the word-processed version. Some students, having completed the word-processed version, were then very keen to look at the texts as set in the coursebook, and to try the accompanying questions, since they had gained the confidence they needed to understand the text through the simplified version.

Modified text

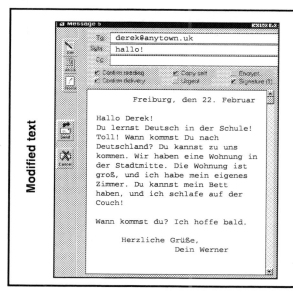

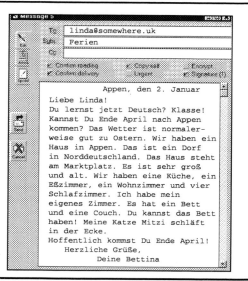

	Werner	Bettina
Wohnt in Freiburg		
Wohnt in Appen		
Hat eine Wohnung		
Hat ein Haus		
Hat sein eigenes Zimmer		
Hat eine Katze		

Modified task

WRITING SKILLS

Two straightforward ways of catering for the differing levels of learners' written skills are:

- valuing differentiated outcomes (see Chapter 1, p7);
- setting graded tasks on a worksheet.

On the following two pages is an example of a differentiated worksheet where tasks are graded in difficulty, for use in a whole class situation:

- Task 1 requires learners to put a tick or a cross in boxes;
- Task 2 requires learners to make a list, in either French or English;
- Task 3 requires learners to complete sentences by filling in gaps;
- Task 4 requires learners to write sentences based on a model;
- Task 5 requires learners to write their own sentences and is open-ended.

Learners could work through the sheet at their own pace. Not all learners would be expected to complete all the tasks.

We have looked at ways in which teachers can begin to address the issue of differentiation, and the ideas and examples referred to are all practical ways forward which can be adopted without a radical change in teaching style or classroom management. Everyone should aim to **start small**, by targeting one class to begin with, in order to monitor and evaluate, as in an action research model. The very fact of being aware of the need of differentiation in the classroom, of recognising that an average class is made up of 25–30 individuals with differing needs and abilities and of valuing the contributions made by all students is an important first step in getting started.

C*i*LT

LES COURS

nom _____

Sylvie parle de ses cours:

J'aime les sciences et les maths. Je n'aime pas l'anglais, le français, l'histoire et la géographie. J'aime l'éducation physique aussi, et le dessin. Je n'aime pas du tout les travaux manuels.

1. Coche, comme ça (✓) si Sylvie aime le cours, et comme ça (✘) si elle n'aime pas le cours.

    ☐ les sciences   ☐ la géographie

    ☐ les maths   ☐ l'éducation physique

    ☐ l'anglais   ☐ le dessin

    ☐ le français   ☐ les travaux manuels

    ☐ l'histoire

Jacques parle de ses cours:

J'aime le français mais je n'aime pas l'anglais. J'aime beaucoup le sport, l'éducation physique, la géographie, les travaux manuels et la cuisine. Je déteste les maths et les sciences aussi. J'adore surtout le dessin.

2. Fais une liste de ce que Jacques aime et n'aime pas.
    A choix, en français ou en anglais.

    Jacques ☺ aime: Jacques ☹ n'aime pas:

    _____   _____

    _____   _____

    _____   _____

    _____   _____

    _____   _____

    _____   _____

LES COURS (suite)

3. Voici des élèves français:
    Qu'est-ce qu'ils aiment? Qu'est-ce qu'ils n'aiment pas? Remplis les blancs. . .

J'_ _ _ _
le
f_ _ _ ç_ _ _

Agnès

Moi, _' _ _ _ _
l'_ _ _ c_ _ _ _ _
p_ _ _ _ q_ _

Vincent

J'_ _ _ _
beaucoup
l_ _ m_ _ _ _

Katie

Je n'_ _ _ _
p_ _ les
s_ _ _ _ c_ _

Pierre

Je n'_ _ _ _
_ _ _ _ _
g_ _ g_ _ _ _ _

Madeleine

4. A toi maintenant — invente deux exemples:

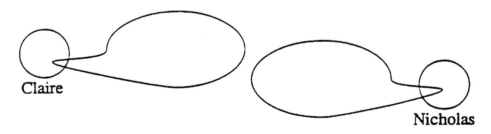

Claire

Nicholas

5. Et toi? Qu'est-ce que **tu** aimes comme matières?
    Qu'est-ce que **tu** n'aimes pas?

    e.g. *J'aime l'anglais. Je n'aime pas les maths.*

    _____

    _____

CiLT

3   Differentiation supported by ICT

As MFL teachers are responsible for delivering parts of the ICT National Curriculum, the role of ICT in enhancing and supporting MFL learning becomes increasingly more important.

ICT is one resource amongst many, which can support learning. However, its flexibility and potential in encouraging both teachers and students to work in a differentiated context are far reaching, in that it allows teachers to adapt simple and more complex language tasks alike to suit the different needs of learners. It allows students access to unprecedented information and communication networks which, when used effectively, can cater for individual needs, interests and styles.

We take as our starting point various classroom activities which could provide differentiated learning opportunities and then go on to illustrate how these might be enhanced by using ICT. It is not within the scope of this Pathfinder to give details of specific applications, but rather to encourage MFL departments to integrate ICT in both short and longer term planning. This will assist them and their students in organising differentiated learning experiences. For those who are already experienced users or for those wishing to experiment further, we recommend specific references in the bibliography.

WORDSEARCHES — VARIATIONS ON A FAMILIAR THEME!

Both student and teacher-generated wordsearches have become 'standard' vocabulary puzzles. The teacher could differentiate these as follows:

- use the same wordsearch for all students — differentiation would be by outcome or speed;
- give learners different puzzles based on the same topic (or a variety of topics for revision): differentiation would be by extent of vocabulary;
- ask students to create wordsearches for each other based on:
  - vocabulary to be learned (e.g. select up to 20 words from a list of 40);
  - vocabulary and spellings to be reinforced (either for an individual or the whole class);
  - homework or revision;
  - personal interest activities.

By using a software package, wordsearches can be created much more quickly, thus allowing for a more profitable use of time. Word Games for Windows (AVP) also available on Acorn, is one such example. It contains two hundred files of words in five different languages: English, French, German, Spanish and Italian, as well as the possibility for teachers to write their own files. The package offers a range of vocabulary-learning games, including a wordsearch, and teachers can choose from a range of differentiation options such as distractors, clues, levels of difficulty and different puzzle sizes.

MATCHING ACTIVITIES

Activities which require students to match one set of items with another are commonplace in the languages classroom, for example:

- matching pictures with words/phrases;
- matching vocabulary items in two languages;
- matching sentence openings with endings;
- matching symbols/pictures to sounds;
- matching written word to sound.

However, such activities can be more fully exploited and more easily differentiated by using ICT to support them. Those teachers who have access to a Concept Keyboard[1] to use with a computer might wish to experiment with packages such as *Concept Match (Blue file)*. This can be used to match pictures, words or phrases on the keyboard with messages on the screen. The teacher has the flexibility to differentiate by creating both the overlays for the keyboard and the screen messages at different levels of complexity (see example of *Toutes Directions/Touch Explorer Plus,* Figure 5, page 24).

If the Concept Keyboard is used with a word bank, it enables all students to create imaginative written tasks, which can gradually build up from picture sequencing to complex poetry writing. Indeed, if typing in words on a normal keyboard is a slow process for some students, then using a word bank (which in itself can be simple or complex) with a Concept Keyboard will dramatically speed up the process and will help to motivate pupils.

---

1   The Concept Keyboard was originally thought of more as an enabling device for the least able. However, as teachers experiment more, it is clear that the keyboard can be of great use with learners of all abilities.

C*i*LT

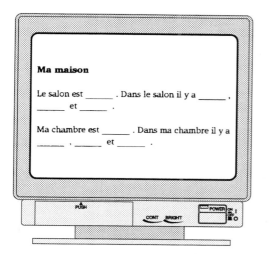

Sample of cloze text displayed on screen with the word bank on the Concept Keyboard overlay. Students move the words and insert them into the text. The word bank can easily become a 'phrase' bank.

Alternatively, the *Language Master* with its strips of card and magnetic tape can provide excellent support for matching sounds (individual words, phrases or short sentences) with either images or the written word. These are available commercially (e.g. those which accompany courses such as *Route Nationale, OK!*) or blank cards can also be purchased, to allow both teachers and learners greater flexibility.

LANGUAGE EXERCISES — CLOZE, UNJUMBLING, SEQUENCING, ETC.

Language exercises used in class are often based on stimulus from a textbook or printed material, which might not always cater for the different needs of individuals or be entirely appropriate in content. By using an authoring package, teachers have the flexibility to create language exercises quickly and effectively using the computer and base them on their own short texts or stimulus geared to their own learners' needs.

For example, *Fun with Texts* (Camsoft) allows teachers (or learners) to have full control over the type and level of text(s) available, including, in *Fun with Texts*, the possibility of pasting directly from the internet. It is straightforward to create short texts on the same topic but at different levels. In addition, differentiation is built into the problem-solving options available, using the same text. Such programs allow created texts to be transformed into problem-solving activities such as text reconstruction, gap-filling, sequencing and decoding. Authoring means that the teacher can ensure that the content is meaningful and the level is appropriate. These packages provide instant feedback and differentiate by time available and support provided, as well as level of difficulty. The following example shows a teacher-generated text based on the topic of daily routines. The first screen shows the teacher-created text and the second screen shows an example of some text with gaps.

Ma routine journalière

Normalement je me réveille vers sept heures et demie du matin. Je me lève tout de suite et je vais dans la salle de bains pour me doucher. Après m'être douchée je m'habille dans ma chambre avant de descendre dans la cuisine pour prendre le petit déjeuner. D'habitude je prends une grande tasse de café et deux tranches de pain.

Je quitte la maison à huit heures vingt et j'arrive au collège à neuf heures moins vingt-cinq. Ce n'est pas très loin!

Les cours commencent à neuf heures moins dix et chaque leçon dure une heure. La recréation est à onze heures et quart, puis on a encore une leçon avant la pause déjeuner. Normalement je mange à la cantine. Puis les cours recommencent à une heure vingt-cinq et finissent à trois heures vingt. Je rentre chez moi vers quatre heures et je fais mes devoirs tout de suite.

ciLT

Text supplied by Cardine Tomlinson, Bramcote Hills School Nottingham.

INFORMATION HANDLING ACTIVITIES

Pupils spend a large proportion of their time in foreign language classrooms engaged in information handling activities. Ranging from question and answer routines, comprehension work and using authentic texts, to carrying out surveys using databases and downloading from the Internet — the possibilities are numerous, since these tasks are rooted in communication. It is of particular interest then to modern languages teachers in their delivery of the curriculum to become familiar with some information handling activities which can be differentiated and supported by technology.

Touch Explorer Plus is a sophisticated information handling package operating at up to six different levels. Each square or group of squares on the Concept Keyboard can contain up to six different messages. Therefore, a series of overlays could involve learners in activities which gradually become more challenging — or different overlays can be targeted at different groups of students. For instance, when devising a guided tour of a town, the overlay of a shopping centre can provide information at successive levels about shops, items sold, offers, prices, conversations and so on. The program can also be exploited for sequencing activities such as instructions or recipes, and it gives information ranging from simple to complex. A simple school timetable could provide graded responses from one word to complete sentences, for example, from: *Deutsch* to *Ich habe montags um zwei Uhr Deutsch.*

It is possible to purchase some ready-made differentiated overlays, such as *Toutes Directions* which supports the French course *Route Nationale* but which can also be used independently.

The overlays have been designed to provide differentiated tasks (by text and outcome). Students choose the level at which they work. The example below shows eight young people and some typical birthday presents.

RT (Level 1)   gives the names of the items and is a picture/word matching exercise

RD (Level 2)   concentrates on who the presents are for and from.

A (Level 3)   provides additional information about the items such as cost and material.

Level 4 (i)   is the help level providing additional information and support such as meanings to words/phrases.

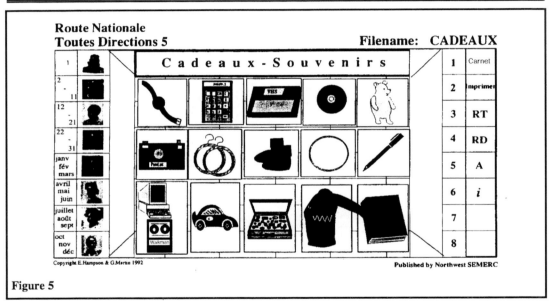

Figure 5

Students can easily move from level to level. Alternatively, by using whitener, the teacher could blank out the choice squares, to ensure that different learners work at different levels but use the same stimulus. If used with a computer, texts created by learners can be put into the notebook *(Carnet)* and transferred to the word-processor. Follow-up activities based on text manipulation could allow for further differentiated tasks (ranging from selecting keywords to changing the third person singular into the first) and the texts can be printed *(Imprimer)*. *Touch Explorer Plus* can also be programmed to provide different types of information to serve as a simple database.

MFL can make a useful contribution by ensuring students use simple databases to present information collected. The Internet is an information source whose potential has yet to be fully realised in the MFL classroom. In the short-term however, it is a good source of differentiation by text. Search engines also allow students to access information in the foreign language. Whilst using the Internet can be both motivating and engaging, departments may wish to focus on its use as a tool for differentiating. The following issues are suggested for 'starters' for discussion:

- role of student e-mail communication (concise style, less emphasis on error, immediacy of message);
- development of students' skills in effective information processing;
- role of teacher-set tasks based on information gathered (N.B. are these **always** necessary?);
- implications of student willingness to access texts 'beyond' current level of linguistic competence;
- range of content available — its authenticity and 'global' nature.

Response activities which require learners to use the information lend themselves in particular to differentiation by task, as in the following example:

DATA: ITEMS HANDED IN AT A LOST PROPERTY OFFICE IN A PARTICULAR WEEK

Students could:

- identify objects by matching 'photographs' with data;
- fill in a simple grid;
- fill in a complex grid;
- write a report giving details of specific lost items;
- develop dialogues between claimant and employee.

It is not only teachers who create the databases, but students must also be encouraged to create their own, based on individual data collection. One example would be a class survey of leisure activities. Teachers and students agree on the fields — *sport, lecture, cinéma, danse*, etc. Most programs support foreign characters and have the facility of allowing data to be entered as pre-set choices. Data collected could be the result of different activities. Some students write words or phrases, others numbers or symbols — a database has the potential to give all learners an opportunity to contribute. The end result, once printed as a table, graph, pie chart, etc, can be used for a variety of follow-up activities.

MULTI-SKILL TASKS

Whilst many of the examples concentrate particularly on reading and writing skills, teachers may wish to encourage their learners to engage in multi-skill activities. Here is an example of how a multi-skill activity can be organised, using a computer and Concept Keyboard, to provide differentiated learning opportunities.

This example combines speaking, listening and reading:

> Students work in pairs. Student A sees and manipulates the keyboard but cannot see the screen. Student B can only see the screen. Half the overlay has a series of squares marked Q1, Q2, Q3, each of which when pressed reveals a question on the screen. This is read out aloud by B and in return A has to select an appropriate answer from the remaining squares on the overlay. This reveals an answer to B, who after reading it aloud decides whether it is correct.

Clearly, the questions as well as the answers can be pitched at different levels and become gradually more complex or more open-ended.

CD-ROM

There is a huge growth in availability of CD-Rom ranging from authentic resources to teaching materials, from *Living Books* to visits to the Louvre, from virtual classrooms to those with sound support and video clips.

However, as a guiding principle, the issues are:

- how might this resource enhance student learning?
- can it provide differentiated learning opportunities?

An example such as *Autolire* (Harper Collins) provides a bank of hundreds of French reading texts at three different levels, based on NC Areas of Experience. The reading texts are supported by sound, image, a word search and dictionary facility as well as activities to develop reading strategies. Students can access the texts independently and select material according to personal interest and ability. As Atkinson (1992) points out:

> 'Through the use of IT we can create a self-contained learning resource which offers students as much or as little support as they require. Such a fully differentiated environment empowers learners to direct their own classroom learning.'

Moreover, the support referred to is not in this case human!

WRITING IN THE FOREIGN LANGUAGE

Wordprocessing has the potential to allow all students to create accurate and legible work in the target language. Most wordprocessing packages contain accented characters with a variety of font sizes and styles. Consequently, the presentation of students' work can now be of the same high quality regardless of level. This clearly helps motivate and support students with a wide range of special needs (including slow or poor handwriters). Some wordprocessing packages enable learners to use word files or banks, for example, students writing letters or postcard messages can select from word banks offering support ranging from individual items of vocabulary to whole phrases. Draft and redrafting facilities also provide valuable support.

Prompt/Writer (Becta) are two simple wordprocessing packages which can be used with either the Concept Keyboard or an ordinary keyboard, or both. Packages such as these allow word sets to be placed in colour coded boxes. In this way, colour coded vocabulary can help with matching questions and answers, and assist with gender, key words and difficult spellings. However, the different coloured boxes can also be used at differentiated levels so that at one level a box might contain keywords, at another additional phrases/structures and so on.

Phases #3 (SEMERC) is a wordprocessing package which differentiates by the support it provides in terms of text size. By a simple click, text size can be changed. This device has great potential for differentiation, for example, students who need to work on shorter texts could have them displayed in larger type — this could provide essential visual (and psychological) support.

DTP

If students are working on producing a newspaper or bulletin, different contributions at different levels can be transformed into an attractive publication by using a desk top publishing (DTP) package.

The aim of this chapter has been to suggest some basic links between ITC and MFL which make the process of differentiation more motivating, varied and flexible. There are currently many good, practical guides to different ICT applications (for example, the CILT InfoTech series) as a manageable tool to support MFL teaching and learning. However, when this support facilitates differentiated learning opportunities, then its role is of paramount importance in realising the potential of ICT in our classrooms.

4   Keeping going

For beginning teachers the initial stages of differentiation tend to focus on individual lessons. Having taken some simple first steps in differentiating, what are the issues which need to be addressed so that differentiation becomes embedded into the teaching repertoire? A look at some points raised by experienced teacher colleagues might be helpful:

DEPARTMENTAL ORGANISATION

Just as individual teachers can introduce differentiation by targeting one class at a time, so a department when working together as a team could target one topic of work at a time. A gradual approach would allow time for reflection and evaluation, in order to incorporate any modifications or improvements into the next topic. The NCC Non-Statutory Guidance (1992) suggested that *'differentiation becomes part of classroom practice from the start of Year 7'*. The Head of Department may decide that some form of in-service training is needed to support the development of differentiation. This may include: visits to other schools to observe lessons and share practice, time to devote to the planning of differentiated activities and the creation or adaptation of materials, or attendance at an externally organised in-service course.

PREPARATION AND PLANNING

Since effective differentiation is a key element in raising levels of motivation and achievement, many MFL departments may wish to examine carefully their departmental policy. Colleagues can then look at how a topic is to be broken down into units of work and individual lessons. Further decisions need to be made concerning where, when and how differentiation is to take place, which activities lend themselves to be differentiated and the type of differentiation to be used most effectively.

The NSG suggested that planning for differentiation could take place on three levels:

- Core objectives
- Reinforcement objectives
- Extension objectives

The core objectives were intended for all students in a class, the reinforcement objectives were intended to give some learners more intensive practice, whilst the extension objectives were to take some students a stage further on.

It should be noted, however, that **all students** need more intensive practice at certain times whilst learning a language, just as **all students** need the stimulus of extension work in order to experience the challenge of moving forwards.

An alternative approach would be to consider differentiation in the following way, for all learners:

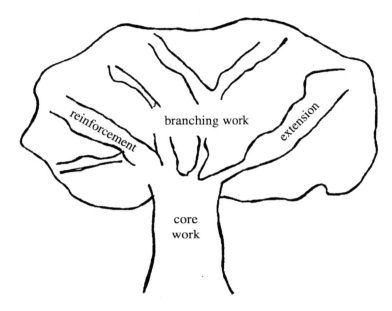

Branching work, namely extension and reinforcement, grows out of core work, taking into account the individual goals, interests and needs of each learner. It follows that unit and lesson planning will include decisions regarding effective delivery of core material, and matching this to the needs of the students.

PLANNING A UNIT OF WORK

Working as a team, departmental colleagues may find it helpful to use a differentiation planning matrix (see page 31) to provide an overview of a particular unit of work, for inclusion in a departmental scheme of work. In this way, a broad picture is obtained at the macro level, which will then lead to the planning of individual lessons at the micro level.

DIFFERENTIATION PLANNING MATRIX

Year _____   Language _____   Unit of work _____

	CORE (All students MUST)	BRANCHING (Most students SHOULD) (Some students MIGHT)	OPPORTUNITIES FOR ASSESSMENT
CONTENT • new language • revision points • cultural information • grammar			
SKILLS • listening • speaking • reading • writing • other (dictionary, etc)			
ICT • using IT • communicating and handling information • controlling, measuring, modelling			
ATTITUDES • cooperation • independence • tolerance • other			
NATIONAL CURRICULUM • POS Part 1 Opportunities • Part II AOE	Notes		Attainment targets: Expected levels AT 1 AT 2 AT 3 AT 4

CiLT

Differentiation and individual learners — 31

Differentiated lesson objectives can be expressed in terms of **learning outcomes**, as follows:

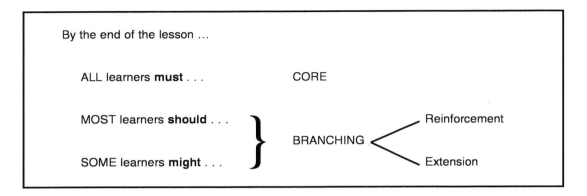

Building differentiation into lesson objectives ensures that a range of opportunities is available to students. At the end of the lesson, the teacher can check whether or not the objectives have been met.

One idea for identifying where differentiation is to occur in a lesson is to use a symbol on the plan, for example in a distinctive colour. The lesson plan (Figure 6) on page 33 is an example of a lesson in which differentiation occurred, and was written by a student teacher.

CLASSROOM MANAGEMENT

Much has already been written about the relationship between successful learning and effective classroom management, which it is not necessary to repeat here. However, there are two important points worth making in the context of differentiation, regarding **group work** and the **use of teacher time**.

GROUP WORK

If students have no experience of working in groups, they will need to learn how to organise themselves efficiently, get out the resources required, co-operate and listen to each other speaking. It may be necessary to establish ground rules at the beginning, so that students agree as to the best ways of proceeding. It is worth spending sufficient time setting up the procedures for working, since it will facilitate quicker progress later on.

LESSON PLAN: INTRODUCTION OF A NEW UNIT OF WORK

Aim	• To introduce new unit of work on schools
Objectives	• By the end of the lesson . . .

- ALL students must recognise and understand the new vocabulary in spoken and written form
- MOST students should be able to produce the new vocabulary in spoken and written form
- SOME students might be able to use the new language in simple sentences in spoken and written form

Preparation
- Make flashcards
- Devise pair work cards/sheets
- Write differentiated worksheet
- Prepare back-up materials

Materials
- Number cards, Blu-tack, white board marker, rubber.

METHOD

Start of lesson
- Presentation of flashcards

Activities
- Teacher-directed question/answer based on flashcards ⚠D
- Pairwork (cards displayed with numbers round room) ⚠D
- Further teacher-directed question/answer using ☺ *j'aime* and ☹ *je n'aime pas* ⚠D
- Pairwork with cue cards ⚠D
- Differentiated worksheet ⚠D

Conclusion
- Miming game

Homework
- *students write out their own timetable in French*

Back-up materials
- Wordsearch
- Crossword

EVALUATION: _____

_____

_____

Figure 6

EXAMPLE OF DIFFERENTIATED GROUP WORK

A short dialogue is given out to students, working in groups of four (or however many roles are required by the dialogue). The dialogue can be taken from a course book or any published resource, as appropriate, or can be written for the purpose by the teacher. This example will work in any language. Students are asked to decide who takes which role, and to read the dialogue through once, aloud. Alternatively, the teacher can allocate roles.

Here is an example of a dialogue based on a café topic:

AU CAFÉ

YVES	*Alain, qu'est-ce que tu prends?*
ALAIN	*Un café , s'il te plaît.*
YVES	*Bon. Trois cafés , s'il vous plaît, Madame.*
SYLVIE	*Non, un jus d'orange pour moi, s'il te plaît.*
YVES	*Bon … alors, deux cafés et un jus d'orange .*
SERVEUSE	*Tout de suite, Monsieur.*

Students then have to continue reading the dialogue aloud, but each time one student should attempt to learn his or her role by heart, and should place their script face down, and read it out without reference to the text. Students continue reading until everyone has learnt their role off by heart. This should require the dialogue to be read five times, including the initial reading.

As each group finishes the learning by heart task, the teacher can begin to add further tasks leading to differentiation, as follows (they can either be written on the board or an OHT, or the teacher may tell each group separately, as appropriate):

Tasks leading to differentiation:

- change items in boxes
- as above, and add something, for example, order a snack, ask where the toilets are
- as above, but create a problem, for example, the coffee machine has broken down
- groups record own dialogues

Different groups of students will work at different paces and will produce very different outcomes from the original dialogue. It is interesting for groups to listen to what each other has produced. Alternatively, if groups have recorded their new dialogues, the recordings can be used in a subsequent lesson as a listening activity. In our experience, this example has always worked well, in that it allows the teacher to have an initial input and then to gradually step back, so that the students can take more control and decide what they want to say for themselves.

Figure 7

It is the teacher's responsibility to create an effective working atmosphere in the classroom, where it is accepted that different students are working at different levels or on different tasks and where each learner's contribution is valued and accepted by everybody.

It should be noted, however, that where group work or carousel work is organised in a classroom it does not necessarily mean that differentiated learning is taking place. For differentiation to take place, the students must be meaningfully engaged in challenging tasks whilst working at their own pace and level at least for some of the time. Figure 7 on page 34 shows an example of differentiated group work, which has been tried and tested successfully with a range of different classes over a number of years.

USE OF TEACHER TIME

If organising for differentiation involves students in working in different combinations of groupings, careful thought must be given to an effective use of the teacher's time and the variety of roles he or she can fulfil: as supporter, assessor, facilitator and co-learner. The teacher also needs to develop a strategy for managing on-task supervision of students, to ensure that they cover an appropriate amount of work each lesson. This will include careful record keeping, both by the teacher and the students, discussions with individual learners on their progress, and spending equal amounts of time with all students over a period of time.

RESOURCES

The resource implications can be considered under three main headings: **provision**, **organisation** and **access**.

PROVISION OF EQUIPMENT

Departments might like to consider the sort of equipment needed in order to allow groups or individual learners to work more independently, for example:

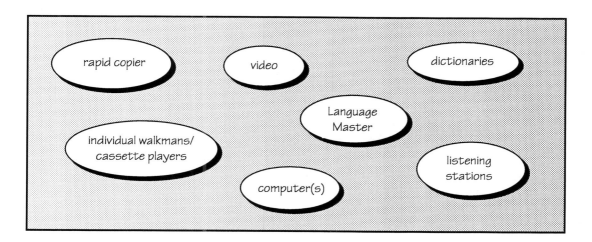

ORGANISATION OF MATERIALS

Many existing materials can be used or adapted when planning differentiated materials; it is not necessary to spend vast amounts of time in making completely new resources. Tasks from course books may be differentiated already, especially in the case of the new courses written since the introduction of the NC. In other cases, texts may be suitable for use, but the tasks that go with them may need adapting, for example by simplifying or enriching. Alternatively, the texts themselves may need simplifying or rewriting, depending on the students' needs. Single copies of textbooks can be very useful when learners work independently. Learners could be asked to look up various references in different books, or extracts could be photocopied for use by several learners. Another useful idea is the organisation of a resource bank, or 'differentiation box' in which various authentic documents, realia, articles and items of interest can be kept in clear plastic wallets, with accompanying tasks or notes. These can then be used by students if they have completed a task or to achieve differentiation by interest. A careful recording system should be developed so that students can provide evidence of materials used and tasks completed.

ACCESS TO RESOURCES

The most important aspect is the way resources are organised to allow equal access to all students. Where only one computer is available, for example, students should be encouraged to use it on a rota-basis. Furthermore, if students are encouraged to develop the skills of working independently, then an easily accessible supply of dictionaries and other reference books and materials is desirable. Students should also be encouraged to work independently in the school library, to access foreign language materials, books, CD-Roms and the Internet.

ASSESSMENT

The assessment of learning has always concerned teachers, but never more so than at present in the light of current changes and developments.

The introduction of the National Curriculum brought differentiation into sharper focus. With eight defined levels and optional summative assessment procedures for MFL in place at the end of Key Stage 3, a major focus lies in the here and now and the formative processes in Key Stages 3 and 4, namely what goes on in classrooms on a daily basis and how it is monitored and assessed.

The GCSE, which falls at the end of Key Stage 4, is currently based on a broadly differentiated format by ability between foundation and higher levels in each of the four skills. Coursework for the GCSE involves students in submitting assignments where '*differentiation will be by outcome and not by task*' (NEAB). The syllabus also adds that it is not a requirement for candidates in one teaching group to work on different assignments with different source materials, but that it will depend on the interests, abilities, approaches and resources of all those concerned.

The NSG stated that '*formative assessment is a continuous process and integral to all teaching and learning*'. It follows, therefore, that if students are involved in differentiated tasks, assessment procedures must take account of these. In a differentiated context, the assessment strategies selected by the teacher (or the students) should not only reflect the language learning experience of individual learners, but also be appropriate for assessment purposes. This very notion has challenged the traditional view of what constitutes evidence of learning, so that if students have been engaged in core and differentiated branching activities, it would not be appropriate to set the same end of topic 'test' for all, if it did not include differentiated assessment opportunities.

Assessment procedures adopted by MFL departments in different schools will vary according to departmental policy. However, the implications of providing differentiated assessment opportunities are challenging.

The following points have been selected from a wide range of assessment issues since they relate specifically to differentiation. Departments may find it a useful catalyst to brainstorm, discuss and prioritise the following suggestions whilst experimenting with their own strategies.

Differentiation and . . .

- formal tests;
- continuous assessment or class-based tests;
- recording individual progress;
- marking procedures;
- homework setting;
- evidence of work;
- GCSE coursework.

The suggestions which follow have been collected from teachers working in a wide range of schools. These ideas arose from discussions during student teacher supervision visits to local schools and are based on sharing successes and concerns regarding differentiation and its implications for assessment. Above all, the consensus was that the provision of differentiated learning opportunities necessarily involves the development of appropriate assessment techniques.

Differentiation and GCSE Coursework

A view from Anthony Gell School, Wirksworth, Derbyshire

'Our first experience of written coursework for MFL has been overwhelmingly positive. It has brought MFL into line with other subjects at GCSE and thus raised its comparative standing in students' eyes.

'The coursework assignments are short and thus less susceptible to an often-levied criticism of "differentiation by advantage", where students enjoy favourable conditions at home, with a wealth of resources not available to all.

'It is possible for students to produce a varied portfolio of work wholly within lesson time. Some of our students have worked effectively in this way, others have been able to organise their time much more independently.

'With our fully comprehensive intake, the coursework has enabled all students to achieve in the writing element, rather than relying on memory. During moderation, it was a pleasure to see the work produced by the full range of students.'

Students' point of view

The coursework has been well-received by students for a variety of reasons:

- all are able to achieve at their own level;
- they can extend their achievement by being aware of the criteria for success at a higher level;
- the brevity compared to other subjects, working to shorter deadlines;
- equality of access to resources;
- some element of choice in assignment;
- direct relevance of work;
- motivation of amassing points towards a grade rather than reliance on 100% terminal examination.

Teachers' point of view

The coursework has been well-received by teachers because:

- certain assignments, for example, an account of work experience, differentiate more effectively by outcome than others, for example, a CV and letter of application;
- as teachers, we need to ensure our students maximise their potential with appropriate guidance regarding the type of assignment most suited to different learning styles, interests and communicative competencies.

Lindsey Smethem and Pam Taylor
Joint Heads of Department

> **"** *I decide when to turn a class activity into an assessed one especially for oral work. In much the same way as primary teachers do when they hear pupils read, then I have started to operate a similar system — every time I listen to a student, or pairs of students, I record this in their individual wallets. At times it is arbitrary but we are currently working on creating a more systematic framework. It does mean that learners are given a chance — whatever their ability — not all the tasks are the same. Afterwards I jot down a reference for the activity and sometimes relate it back to an attainment level.* **"**

> **"** *In class, I think it's important to give learners different types of support — even when the activity is used as an assessment task. For a listening task, I might allow students to listen as often as they need to. They then note the number of times they listened on their record sheet. Students are no longer competing against each other but their performance is being matched by graded levels.* **"**

> **"** *I set core homework (at least once a week) and students set their own branching homework (usually one or two per two weeks). They keep a strict record of this in their folder/progress sheets. I was surprised that it wasn't the headache I'd envisaged — keeping track of homework set by students. Spot checks are also useful.* **"**

> **"** *We spent a lot of time re-designing our student topic checklists to turn tick boxes into differentiated targets. For example, one box might read* Je sais compter 1–10, *the next box might read* Je sais compter 1–20. *This means that individual learners will tick different boxes. The completed checklists are then placed into the learners' own wallets at the end of the topic. I think we are helping the students by fine-tuning the targets — making them more differentiated.* **"**

> ❝ *We invested a lot of time at the very beginning setting up our ground rules for assessment. All our Year 7 students are fully aware of what we expect them to do as far as homework and assessed work are concerned. They are also aware of the importance of their personal portfolio — this is where they transfer selected pieces of work with help from us, as evidence of progress at the end of every topic. We have noticed a real difference between the way Year 7s respond to assessment and other year groups.* ❞

> ❝ *In our department we have divided assessment into two categories — formative assessment (class-based including homework) and formal/summative assessment (departmental/Year-based).*
>
> *The starting point for formative assessment is the classroom. It's up to individual teachers to select a series of class activities in all four skill areas to be used as assessments – based on the topic and the course book, tapes and worksheets. These are kept in separate plastic envelopes in a large tub. These assessment tasks are differentiated as follows:*
>
> (i) *students choose to do them when they feel ready;*
>
> (ii) *not all students will complete the whole range of all assessment tasks but all students should attempt those with a red sticker (core or basic tasks);*
>
> (iii) *students tick their names on sheets displayed on the classroom wall to show when they have successfully completed an assessment. The completed task when marked is filed in the individual's personal wallet;*
>
> (iv) *reading, writing and listening tasks are often marked by the students, using answer sheets. Students are also encouraged to mark each other's work. However, for each task we have developed the idea of* à l'aide *envelopes which contain additional support for students. On completion students sign on the back to say whether or not they did it with or without extra help. To date they have been really honest – they enjoy having that responsibility.*
>
> *The starting point for summative assessment is different. One member of the department is responsible for each topic. Using National Curriculum AT level descriptions, assessment tasks are devised which cater for a wide range of ability. They tend to get progressively harder. We are still working on this. All classes in the year do these.* ❞

> *At the front of the class folder containing individual progress sheets,(see example below) I have placed at the beginning of every topic, a list of core activities which I expect everyone to have covered and a range of others from which individuals might select. These are also displayed on the wall.*

SAMPLE INDIVIDUAL PROGRESS SHEET

ACTIVITÉ CHOISIE	DATE	ACCOMPLIE	DATE	REMARQUES

> *Each student has his or her own cassette tape. The tape also provides evidence of work. I find this really useful for recording my own personal comments and messages to individuals. At first I used to try to mark all the tapes at once – this took ages. I now select about a third at any one time. Learners know that I will listen to their tapes but they are never sure when. This is now more manageable.*

It is appropriate at this point to examine more closely the role of differentiation within the National Curriculum.

5   Differentiation and the National Curriculum

The framework of the National Curriculum, namely the Programmes of Study (PoS) and the Attainment Targets (ATs), should provide the teacher with a means of obtaining detailed knowledge of the attainment of every student, through careful recording of achievement and thorough documentation. This will enable the teacher to demonstrate the progression through the ATs of all students in the group.

The Non-Statutory Guidance referred to four types of progression:

- progression in content;
- progression in skills;
- linguistic progression;
- progression in development of cultural awareness.

Progression is achievable through the delivery of the PoS, and measurable through the reporting framework of the ATs.

Given that there are eight defined levels for MFL, plus an additional level for exceptional performance, it is conceivable that in any one given year students will have reached widely different levels of attainment in all four ATs. In Year 9, for example, in a mixed-ability class, some pupils may be at Level 2, whilst other pupils may have reached Level 6 or beyond (in the case of bilingual students). The implications of such a situation can appear far-reaching, which is why 'an understanding of progression in the ATs is essential for planning differentiated work' (NCC February 1992).

A brief examination of the ATs and the level descriptions on the following pages will illustrate how the concepts of differentiation and progression can be linked using examples of mixed-ability classes from various years.

It would seem that the most effective way to achieve progression is by providing differentiated learning tasks based on clearly-defined targets. One student teacher, reflecting on the issue of how to cater for the wide ability range in her classroom, commented that differentiation was *the only way to satisfy the demands of both the National Curriculum and the learners*.

CiLT

AT1   **LISTENING AND RESPONDING**
Topic   School subjects
Activity   Recording of a student from a link school describing a specific school day
Year   7

NC Level	Description	Specific skill	Task
1	Pupils show understanding of simple classroom commands, short statements and questions. They understand speech spoken clearly, face to face or from a good quality recording, with no background noise or interference. They may require considerable support, such as repetition and gesture.	Identify individual items in a list.	From a longer list of subjects, students tick the ones they hear mentioned.
2	Pupils show understanding of a range of familiar statements and questions, including everyday classroom language and instructions for setting tasks. They respond to a clear model of standard language, but may need items to be repeated.	Identify and understand specific details in familiar utterances.	On an incomplete timetable for the day, students fill in the remaining lessons.
3	Pupils show understanding of short passages, including instructions, messages and dialogues, made up of familiar language spoken at near normal speed but without interference. They identify and note main points and personal responses, such as likes, dislikes and feelings, but may need short sections to be repeated.	Identify and note main points and specific details in short instructions, messages and dialogues.	On a blank timetable, students fill in all the details.

This example is one of differentiation by **task** using the same text for all learners. It could be done as a class exercise, or by students working in groups, or by students working individually. The three separate tasks are all relatively simple to set up.

CILT

AT2   SPEAKING
Topic   Personal Information
Activity   Role Play
Year   8

NC Level	Description	Specific skill	Task
2	Pupils give short, simple responses to what they see and hear. They name and describe people, places and objects. They use set phrases for purposes such as asking for help and permission. Their pronunciation may still be approximate and the delivery hesitant, but their meaning is clear.	Give and find out simple information.	Students work in pairs, using some cue cards with symbols to exchange simple personal information.
3	Pupils take part in brief unprepared tasks of at least two or three exhanges, using visual or other cues to help them initiate and respond. They use short phrases to express personal responses, such as likes, dislikes and feelings. Although they use mainly memorised language, they occasionally substitute items of vocabulary to vary questions or statements.	Adapt memorised words and phrases.	Students work in pairs using same cue cards, but taking on the persona of a famous or imaginary person.
4	Pupils take part in simple structured conversations of at least three or four exchanges, supported by visual or other cues. They are beginning to use their knowledge of language to adapt and substitute single words and phrases. Their pronunciation is generally accurate and they show some consistency in their intonation.	Give a short presentation or prompted talk on everyday activities, interests or future plans.	Students work individually or in pairs to prepare a presentation, either as themselves or as a famous or imaginary person (see above).

This example shows how differentiation can be achieved by **outcome**. All students can start with a basic cue card, and progress at their own pace through the three tasks. Not all students would be expected to attempt the presentation, which is a branching activity to challenge a range of learners, including high achievers, risk takers and those motivated by the task.

C*i*LT

AT3　　READING AND RESPONDING
Topic　　Holidays
Activity　　Various reading tasks
Year　　9

NC Level	Description	Specific skill	Task
3	Pupils show understanding of short texts and dialogues, made up of familiar language, printed in books or word-processed. They identify and note main points, including likes, dislikes and feelings. They are beginning to read independently, selecting simple texts and using a bilingual dictionary or glossary to look up new words.	Understand and respond to texts consisting of short, simple sentences in familiar contexts.	Students read examples of pen-friend letters and select information to complete a grid (see examples on pp14–15).
4	Pupils show understanding of short stories and factual texts, printed or clearly handwritten. They identify and note main points and some details. In their independent reading, in addition to using a bilingual dictionary or glossary, they are beginning to use context to deduce the meaning of unfamiliar language.	Understand and respond to short, factual and non-factual texts, both printed and handwritten, which include sentences containing short clauses and some unfamiliar language.	Students read individual, authentic penfriend letters from link school and compose a reply.
5	Pupils show understanding of a range of written material, including texts covering past, present and future events. They identify and note main points and specific details, including opinions. Their independent reading includes authentic materials, such as information leaflets, newspaper extracts, letters or databases. They are generally more confident in reading aloud, and in their use of reference materials.	Understand and respond to texts, including short narratives, which include some complex sentences and some unfamiliar language, using appropriate reference materials.	Students read an article from an authentic magazine about making new friends on holiday. They then write to the author of the article about their own experiences.

This is an example of differentiation by **text**, with a series of stimuli provided by the teacher. Students could be allocated to each text according to specific criteria, such as interest or ability.

CiLT

AT4   **WRITING**
Topic   Weather
Activity   Various written tasks
Year   10

NC Level	Description	Specific skill	Task
4	Pupils write individual paragraphs of about three or four simple sentences, drawing largely on memorised language. They adapt a model by substituting individual words and set phrases. They are beginning to make appropriate use of dictionaries and glossaries as an aid to memory.	Write a small number of related sentences based on a model, or from memory, to find out and convey simple information, using present tense.	Students write a description of the seasonal weather to send to link school.
5	Pupils produce short pieces of writing in which they seek and convey information and opinions in simple sentences. They refer to recent experience and future plans, as well as to everyday activities. They are beginning to apply basic elements of grammar in new contexts, but there may be a number of mistakes. They use dictionaries or glossaries as an aid to memory and to look up unknown words.	Produce a short piece of continuous writing, consisting of simple sentences, to seek and convey information and opinions, using past or future tense.	Students to describe previous or forth-coming season's weather, including personal opinions and experiences.
6	Pupils write in paragraphs, using simple descriptive language, and refer to past, present and future actions and events. They use both informal and formal styles of writing, such as when keeping a diary, booking accommodation and scripting dialogues. Although there may be some mistakes, the meaning is usually clear.	Use simple descriptive language to write in paragraphs about familiar topics and experiences, using the present, past and future tenses.	Students write an account in response to reading about a weather disaster.

This example shows how differentiation can operate in different ways within the same topic area. If students are allowed to choose their task, differentiation by **interest** will happen. On the other hand, if the teacher allocates the tasks, this could lead to differentiation by **ability**

c*i*LT

or guided choice. Alternatively, each task can be tackled on different levels, resulting in differentiation by **outcome**. This example also demonstrates how grammar can be taught at differentiated levels, taking account of individual learners' confidence and ability to understand and manipulate tenses, in this instance. Some students will be ready before others to use a number of tenses at the same time, and their branching work will therefore need to consist of extension activities to take account of this. Other students will need reinforcement activities in the use of the past tense, for example.

The purpose of this chapter has been to try and demonstrate how differentiation and progression can work in relation to the AT level descriptions of the NC. It is not always a straightforward matter to match a task to a level, and in some ways the examples given in this chapter may appear rather arbitrary. Indeed, teachers may find it impractical at times to set up a number of tasks or to organise a number of different resources in the space of one lesson. As a result of many discussions with teachers over the years, and in our own teaching experience, one of the most straightforward ways of differentiating is where a single, open-ended task is set up, which allows learners to work within it at their own level according to individual needs, and where differentiation by outcome operates.

In the last chapter, we examine ways of moving students forward in their learning, looking at strategies to promote independence.

6   Moving forwards: challenging learners

CREATING A MOTIVATING LEARNING ENVIRONMENT

Experimenting with providing differentiated task types, activities and resources is a useful springboard for a beginning teacher. However, it is only as teachers begin to get to know their students, their individual needs and preferred learning styles, that one can really begin to build up quality relationships and create a differentiated learning environment.

A useful awareness-raising process might focus on two aspects:

* Self as learner
* Self as teacher

SELF AS LEARNER

Departments may wish to begin by looking at themselves as learners. This can be a very powerful process. In a training session[2] with a group of cross-discipline PGCE student teachers, participants filled in an isometric questionnaire *(the Myers-Briggs Type Indicator)* and discussed how their personality 'types' might potentially impact on their own learning. This was followed up by a lesson in Urdu (a 'new' language) which, after an initial teacher input, was centred on a variety of group, pair or individual activities. The student teachers were then consulted as to which activities they had understood and enjoyed most, and were asked to give reasons. The point here was not to label individuals, but to demonstrate how preferred learning styles have a powerful effect on one's attitude to learning and one's motivation to complete the tasks set.

The activities were as follows:

* a group role play;
* a pair work activity matching 'real' foods to the Urdu word and practising correct pronunciation;
* a video sequence where viewers had to pick out specific information;
* a vocabulary learning exercise, choosing words to learn from a list.

The 'learner' consultation was most revealing – especially from those who were not 'linguists':

---

2   Led by Stephen Pugh and Ann Cambier of Derbyshire LEA.

CiLT

> 'I hated being subjected to whole group repetition. I'd rather say the sounds to myself.'
>
> 'I found the teacher's presentation of new foreign sounds very threatening — I couldn't remember them and I panicked.'
>
> 'Watching the video was really boring — my concentration wandered.'

in contrast to:

> 'I really liked the group work — it was good to feel supported by others.'
>
> 'It was easy to remember the new words once we'd handled the food — it was funny.'
>
> 'I liked being given a choice of words to learn and then discussing with other members of the group why they'd chosen their words and how they'd remembered them.'

This process can best be summed up by a comment from one student teacher who said:

> 'This was a startling experience — it put teaching practice into perspective. I now realise that I had expected all my learners to be interested in the work I set, without then considering them as having preferences — like we all have! It was so important to have my awareness raised about the effects of different types of learning experiences to discover that I really did not like some, and others I enjoyed.'

The participants were unanimous in concluding that this experience was important to them as future teachers because:

- it made them aware of themselves as learners;
- it raised issues concerning their preferred teaching styles;
- instead of **labelling** individuals, it made them realise that students will share preferred learning styles, and that these styles have both advantages and disadvantages. They are in fact **equalisers**.

To extend this idea to the Modern Foreign Languages department, teachers may wish to:

- fill in a personality and learning questionnaire — relate the 'results' to personal learning and teaching preferences;
- consult learners in a particular targeted class — by raising student awareness of personal learning styles (through simple tests, quizzes or questionnaires) and find out which activities they really enjoy and why;

REMEMBER! ☞ **All styles are equal**

☞ **All styles have their advantages/disadvantages**

- carry out an audit after a topic of work, to review extending teaching styles further and provision of a variety of activities or other learning opportunities;
- ask learners to evaluate their work not only in terms of progress but also in terms of how they adapted to different activities. Students need to be able to work in various styles whilst being aware of the style that suits them best.

In recent years, there has been a noticeable shift from a concentration on the teacher to the learner. There are several learning preference questionnaires — for example, those based on Kolb's work (see Hart, 1996). He identified four broad stages. Those learners who prefer:

Concrete experiences	Actively involved: • learning by being involved and feeling
Reflective observation	Watchfully engaged: • learning by watching and considering
Abstract conceptualisation	Thoughtfully detailed: • learning by thinking and asking how, why
Active experimentation	Decisively practical: • learning by deciding and doing — testing out ideas

Research indicates that effective learning involves all four of the above stages, yet individuals will place a very different emphasis across the four stages. This gives an overall preferred learning style.

According to any particular activity, learners' preferences may, or may not be satisfied — if they are not, then individuals may need encouragement and reassurance from the teacher. Moreover, individual teachers react to different class teaching situations in different ways. It is therefore recommended that individual teachers within a department examine their own teaching and learning styles in order to explore ways of extending and varying approaches and opportunities. This can indeed provide a very powerful step forward in reviewing the overall potential for providing differentiated teaching and learning contexts within an MFL department.

ENCOURAGING LEARNER INDEPENDENCE

The development of learner autonomy is often referred to as the ultimate learning goal. Autonomy is to do with encouraging learners to take responsibility for their own learning and involves:

- being clear about aims and personal goals;
- having access to a supportive environment;
- making informed choices through learning how to learn;
- contributing to the content, process and assessment of learning.

The link between differentiation and autonomous learning is clearly stated in the National Curriculum Programme of Study Part 1, Section 3c, *'Pupils should be taught to develop their independence in language learning and use'*.

Students should have regular opportunities to:

- work independently of the teacher (on their own and with others);
- use a range of materials and resources;
- use computers;
- develop independence in their choice of tasks, materials and use of equipment.

Teachers who offer some clearly differentiated learning opportunities to their learners are well on the way to building up an environment conducive to the development of learner autonomy. Here are some ways forward:

CiLT

BEING CLEAR ABOUT AIMS AND PERSONAL GOALS

Having discussed the core objectives for a particular topic with students, the teacher could then ask individuals to suggest some personal goals.

- For example, in the topic of sport, the teacher could ask students what they would most like to learn about, to write down their suggestions, to compare the student suggestions with those in the textbook and make joint decisions about **some** elements of the content of the topic.
- Another suggestion might be to ask individual students to brainstorm ten words which they want to learn in the target language when starting a new topic. This is in effect differentiation by interest.

ORGANISING A SUPPORTIVE WORKING ENVIRONMENT

By gradually increasing the variety of teaching and learning opportunities, students will have the flexibility to respond to different experiences and make informed choices. Teachers may find that a gradual shift in emphasis from whole class activities (though still important) to group and paired work is more appropriate as differentiated activities increase. Every third lesson, say, may be organised as a 'branching' lesson, where students have a choice of activities using a variety of materials and equipment.

One teacher displayed on large wall posters the core activities which all students had to tackle, and a range of branching activities from which students could select. Students were given a time limit (three to four weeks) but could choose which branching activities to work on and when. Core work was sometimes tackled through whole class teaching. Another teacher with 90-minute lessons preferred to offer a range of group and paired activities within each lesson.

As teachers build up a bank of differentiated materials, all-important individualised work and student-teacher partnerships will develop. Although successful small group work requires very careful planning, it can give teachers the chance to direct specific work to individuals, nurture learner choice, exploit differentiated work and, more vitally, discuss individual progress. Such teacher-led small group sessions are essential to the development of student independence. Little (1989) calls it 'discretionary time' and encourages teachers to find ways of creating this space with students during a series of lessons.

It might also be useful for teachers to examine closely the quality and organisation of group work. The following checklist can be used in the department as a basis for INSET discussion. The answers to these questions can then lead to an exploration of the type of

CiLT

group activity offered in terms of **variety** and **differentiated opportunities**, and will help teachers in the creation and use of 'discretionary time'.

- How often do my students work in groups?
- How are the groups set up?
- What do the students actually do?
- How is the work differentiated?
- What do I do when students work in groups?
- What do I hope to achieve?
- What do my students think?

It is also recommended that departments analyse the range of classroom tasks and activities in terms of cognitive challenge and appropriacy. Cummins (in Hall, 1995) suggested a simple matrix plotting high-low cognitive demands on one axis and context-reduced embedded demands on the other (page 54). Context-embedded language aids comprehension through a range of support, including photographs, images, diagrams, familiar situations, short responses and frequent redundancies. Context-reduced or unembedded language is more demanding since it is less supported by contextual clues. It tends to involve longer chunks of language, especially written text or abstract discussions which are dense in meaning. Activities which are predominantly context reduced and make low cognitive demands are to be avoided over a sustained period. Such activities include parroting and copying. Plotting MFL tasks on the matrix provides a useful way of ensuring that all learners are 'stretched' rather than mindlessly involved in undemanding time-consuming activities. After all, whatever their abilities and needs, students must be challenged.

LEARNING HOW TO LEARN

Learning how to learn helps individuals, especially less effective learners, to become more efficient and independent. Students who are aware of themselves as learners are more likely to be able to make informed choices which will affect the quality of their experiences. Students who are encouraged to ask – What am I doing? Why? How am I doing it? When? What can it be used for? – are also being encouraged to think about the learning process and accept a share in the responsibility (not always 'comfortable' for the teacher!).

The teacher's role is vital in making learning how to learn **explicit**, to focus the learners' attention on **how** best to learn rather than simply what to learn. Sometimes referred to as 'learner training', this process involves the teacher in assisting learners to select and concentrate on different learning strategies (see Pathfinder 31, *Teaching learners how to learn*).

High cognitive demand

Generalises

Compares and **contrasts**

Summarises

Plans

Classifies by known criteria

Transforms, personalises,
gives information

Recalls and **reviews**

Seeks solutions to problems

Argues a case using evidence persuasively

Identifies criteria, **develops** and **sustains ideas**

Justifies opinion or judgement

Evaluates critically

Interprets evidence, makes deductions

Forms hypotheses, asks further questions
for investigation

Predicts results

Applies principles to new situation

Analyses, suggests solution and tests

◄— Context embedded———(COGNITIVE PROCESSES)———Context unembedded —►

Reading to find specific information
- identifies
- names
- matches
- retells

Transfers information from one medium
to another

Applies known procedures

Describes observations

Sequences

Narrates with sense of beginning,
middle, end

- **parrots**: repeats utterances of adult or peer

- **copies**: reproduces information from board
  or text

Low cognitive demand

c*i*LT

A simple example might be to do with the learning of vocabulary. Teachers could encourage students to experiment with and evaluate different ways of learning vocabulary, for example:

I am better at learning:	Yes	No
By heart	✓	
By regular review/revision		✓
Within a context (phrase, sentence, picture)	✓	
Through using lists in different ways	✓	
Through word groups		✓
With help of music or rhythms		✓
With the help of personal lists	✓	
From a brainstorm session		

Another example might involve information seeking. Teachers could emphasis over a period of time different ways of 'finding things out' using a range of resources or people. At the end of that time, learners could list the different resources and methods in terms of appropriateness and effectiveness. 'Learning how to learn' acknowledges that individuals will need different learning experiences. In the following extract students are actively encouraged to explore alternative ways of learning, not only to increase their own awareness of learning styles, but to enable them to become more effective learners — differentiation plays a key role.

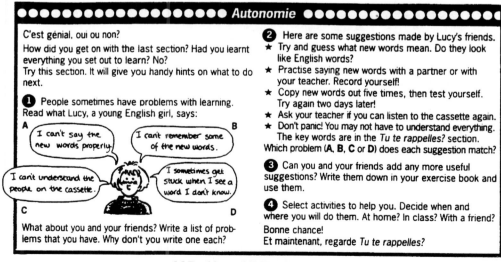

M Buckby and T Huntley, *Auto*

If students are to become confident, independent language learners (whatever their ability), they must feel involved in their own learning. Initially, achieving this may be a question of balance between:

- core and branching work;
- class/group work and individual activities;
- teacher-led and student-led activities;
- teacher-selected and student-selected materials and resources;
- teacher assessment and peer or self assessment;
- free choice and guided choice . . . and so on.

Individual departments can prioritise, select from and add to the list, depending on the teachers' interests and the students they are targeting. However, taking responsibility for their learning and contributing actively to that process may not come 'naturally' to learners. They will need to be taught how to:

- set their own learning goals;
- write an action plan of how they are going to achieve these goals;
- assess their performance;
- evaluate the processes used.

By being involved in these processes, students will become more confident and motivated — whatever their ability — to accept a share in the learning of a foreign language with their teachers and peers. Gradually, individuals will be encouraged to take on more responsibility to direct those processes — which by their very nature will be differentiated — and eventually become independent learners.

If teachers regard the development of student autonomy as an integral part of the teaching and learning process, not only will they involve their learners to a greater extent but also satisfy specific requirements of the National Curriculum.

Educators have always been aware of the need to differentiate. Yet as that understanding increases so, too, does the role played by teachers and learners in defining and refining the nature of differentiation.

Our student teachers, in the early stages of their professional development, highlighted the following key messages and watchpoints as an initial checklist to aid their own learning and to help them during their teaching practice:

KEY MESSAGES

1 Differentiation is about more than differences in ability — there are many other factors which make children different from one another.

2 Not all work needs to be differentiated — CORE work should be accessible to all students.

3 The possibilities for differentiation increase the better you get to know your students.

4 Many teachers differentiate intuitively — it becomes a guiding principle.

5 It is advisable to have extension activities available at all times.

6 When planning a lesson, having differentiated objectives will help to ensure that students are working at appropriate levels.

7 Differentiation occurs through the use of a variety of teaching and learning styles. There are different approaches to, and ways of, differentiating.

8 Differentiation by interest can help motivate reluctant learners.

9 Individual target setting can be an effective way of differentiating by outcome.

WATCHPOINTS

1 When differentiating by outcome, the teacher must have a clear idea of the range of outcomes expected, and must communicate this to the class and/or individuals.

2 Extension work should not be provided only for the more able learners — all learners need extending at times.

3 Similarly, reinforcement work will benefit learners across the ability range at different times.

4 Setting students according to ability does not mean that differentiation becomes unnecessary.

Experienced teachers may wish to carry out an internal audit of their practice within departments by considering the following action plan:

AUDIT OF PRACTICE

Getting started

- Take a critical look at current practice
- Target one group of students
- Create short-term objectives
- Use the four skill areas to select simple tasks

Developing tasks

- Consider range of abilities and interests of students in target group
- Select variety of tasks and match to appropriate way of differentiating
- Investigate possibilities of incorporating ICT
- Have a go at adapting a selection of published materials

Keeping going

- Put it on the agenda: discussion point at departmental meetings
- Share planning and preparation of core/branching work with colleagues
- Experiment with student groupings
- Audit of resources — potential for differentiation?
- Create a differentiated assessment task

Moving forwards

- Long-term objectives: create/develop departmental policy
- Plan and hold INSET day
- Target one group to develop independent learning skills
- Review and evaluate procedures to date

Alternatively, INSET trainers can provide a useful external stimulus for reviewing departmental practice. The following example (pages 59–61) is taken from one such session.

In this Pathfinder we have tried to show how the practice of differentiation has moved forwards in recent years. Hopefully it will continue to do so as our collective understanding and awareness of effective ways of teaching and learning deepens and develops.

CiLT

THE 'WHAT IF?' / 'WHAT NOW?' APPROACH TO HELPING ALL LEARNERS

Broad outline of stages

- Observe your students learning
- Raise your own awareness about what affects learning
- Use your raised awareness to formulate contingency plans for future learning
- Develop ways of reacting on the spot to 'learning blockages'
- Enable your students to improve their learning

HOW TO HELP STUDENTS GET ON WITH A TASK THEY FIND DIFFICULT

There are a number of steps you can take to make an activity/resources more accessible. Quite often teachers adopt more than one of the tactics below in adapting just one activity.

1. Break down the activity into smaller stages

The students do exactly the same as their classmates but the activity is broken into smaller steps.

e.g. *Listening activity*
When you play a tape of a shopping dialogue and ask your class to jot down what the customer buys, you can guide some students to listen out for certain items during each playback.

e.g. *Speaking activity*
When you ask students to take on new identity according to details in symbol form on a cue card, you can direct some students to go around and give only answers to start with and then later to go and ask questions.

e.g. *Reading/Writing activity*
When you ask your students to read a letter and write a reply to it, you can break this down into two explicit stages.

2. Simplify the activity

All students do the same activity, but those who find it difficult have a simpler version.

3. Provide a framework which aids comprehension and acts as a focus for attention

Some students are given a framework which adds context and meaning to the task. It also can help the pupil structure their response.

e.g. When listening to a conversation some students have a grid on which to record the details of the conversation. Those who don't find this difficult, listen and jot down notes.

4. Check the readability of the resource

The teacher can check the layout and presentation of the resource and make it more comprehensible.

- Ensure the print is large, legible and not in block capitals
- Compartmentalise activities
- Take away superfluous information
- Check that you are requiring your students to read from left to right and from top to bottom
- Create more space between blocks of text. Don't overcrowd the resource.

5. Provide visuals to aid meaning

Some students have extra visuals to give them clues about the meaning of what they are hearing or reading.

6. Build in an element of student choice of language, pace etc.

Allow students to choose:

a) the language they produce;

b) the type of support they need;

c) how to set about the task — the order, speed and presentation.

7. Provide a point of reference

Those students who aren't very organised about bringing their books or aren't very efficient at recording their learning in the first place, need extra reference materials to help them to learn and remember new language.

CiLT

HOW TO EXTEND STUDENTS WHO FIND A TASK EASY

There are a number of ways in which you can extend students who you think are finding an activity easy.

1. **Remove the scaffolding that aids meaning**

   Take away the visuals and extra written information.

2. **Increase**

   Reduce the amount of cognates. Increase the length and complexity of sentences.

3. **Make the task more complicated**

4. **Add a twist to the task**

   Put the students under pressure. Make them do the task in a certain time. Make them perform from memory.

5. **Make the task open-ended**

   Allow students to use their imagination and add extras.

6. **Give students the opportunity to infer meaning**

   Challenge them to arrive at meaning of language they haven't met before.

7. **Elicit a longer, more detailed, more accurate response**

8. **Give students opportunities to take risks and to experiment**

   Especially in the area of classroom language.

Janeen Leith

Appendix

This table shows strategies that have been suggested by student teachers in response to a range of differences that they observed during their teaching practice. The strategies are all generic and are not exhaustive. Whilst the strategies suggested by the trainees are basic to good classroom practice, they nonetheless serve as a useful reminder of the complexity of individual differences.

Individual differences	Suggested strategies
Age, maturity	• match activities as carefully as possible to the age and maturity of the students • use printed materials judiciously, matching activities as carefully as possible to the age and maturity of the students – just because it's in a textbook doesn't mean students will find it relevant • •
Gender	• experiment with seating arrangements • direct questions equally to boys and girls • organise activities that oblige students to mix naturally e.g. surveys • •
Physical capabilities	• examine the layout of the classroom for possible mobility difficulties • choose optimum seating arrangements for students with sight or hearing impairment • •
Personality	• find ways of channelling dominant personalities • acknowledge different personalities, their strengths and weaknesses • •

ciLT

Individual differences	Suggested strategies
Preferred learning style	• vary your teaching approach to accommodate a wide variety of interests • •
Self-confidence and self-esteem	• use praise generously, either to individuals or groups, publicly and privately • set some tasks with short-term achievable goals for those lacking in confidence • •
Length of attention span	• have activities of differing lengths • be aware that individuals have differing concentration spans, include appropriate changes of activity in a lesson plan • •
Speed of working	• set tasks which have time limits and give frequent warnings • have extension tasks available • let students finish some tasks in entirety for the satisfaction of finishing • •
Motivation	• find out what motivates different learners and try and incorporate students' ideas where possible • •

ciLT

Individual differences	Suggested strategies
Reputation	• avoid saying, 'Ah, so you're the brother/sister of . . . are you?' • keep an open mind about each student, don't jump to conclusions • •
Behaviour	• have well-planned lessons • use a variety of tasks and resources • take a fresh look at the Elton Report • •
Class relationships	• arrange seating sensitively • be aware of the changing pattern of relationships within the class • •
Social background	• be sensitive to students whose home environment makes it difficult for them to do homework effectively • look for alternative ways of involving students who can't travel abroad in foreign links, for example, e-mail, penfriend exchanges • •
Parental support	• allow students to do their homework at school, if they wish • •

CiLT

Individual difference	Suggested strategies
Outside interests	• find ways of allowing students to share their interests in class • talk to students informally about their interests • •
Prior knowledge	• find out what students already know before starting a new topic, for example, by brainstorming • try to use prior knowledge in a constructive way • •
Cultural differences	• be sensitive and flexible in your reaction to unexpected situations • look for ways of introducing cultural elements into lessons – easy if there are speakers of other languages in the class • •
Students with English as a second language	• exploit the capabilities of bilingual students, for example, by comparing languages • •

The student teachers reached the conclusion that there were three key points to learn from this exercise:

> **VARIETY**
>
> **SENSITIVITY**
>
> **KNOW YOUR STUDENTS**

CiLT

Bibliography

Atkinson T, *Hands Off! It's my go* (CILT/NCET, 1992)

Atkinson T, *WWW The Internet,* InfoTech 3 (CILT, 1998)

Barthorpe T and Visser J, *Differentiation: your responsibility* (NARE, 1991)

Blamire R (ed) *Languages for all – IT in modern language learning for children with special needs* (NCET, 1991)

Buckby M and Huntley T, *Auto – Livre d'etudiant 1* and *Auto 1 – Teacher's resource book* (Collins Educational, 1992)

Convery A and Coyle D, *Differentiation: taking the initiative,* Pathfinder 18 (CILT, 1993)

Dickinson C and Wright J, *Differentiation: a practical handbook of classroom strategies* (National Council for Educational Technology, 1993)

Dickinson L, *Learner autonomy 2: learner training for language learning* (Authentik, 1992)

Differentiating the secondary curriculum package (Wilts CC, 1991) including 21 booklets and video:

    5   *Computers,* Brodie, T and Butterworth, I
    9   *Producing your own educational material,* McAsey, D
    12   *Base lining,* Hill, T
    17   *Assessment: the window on learning,* Hanson, D
    18   *Marking written work,* Garnett, J
    20   *Senior Management team,* Long, L

Diffey N, 'Scottish approach to differentiation', *Language Learning Journal*, No.16 (1997)

Discipline in Schools, Report of the Committee of Enquiry chaired by Lord Elton (HMSO, 1989)

Ellis G and Sinclair B, *Learning to learn English: a course in learner training* (CUP, 1989)

Gathercole I (ed) *Autonomy in language learning* (with video) (CILT, 1992)

George D, *The challenge of the able child* (David Fulton, 1992)

Hall D, *Assessing the Needs of Bilingual Pupils* (David Fulton Publishers, 1995). See Cummins' Framework, pp.49–63.

Harris V, 'Differentiation – not as easy as it seems', *Language Learning Journal 12* (ALL, 1995)

Harris V, *Teaching Learners How to Learn,* Pathfinder 31 (CILT, 1997)

Hart S (ed) *Differentiation and the secondary curriculum: debates and dilemmas* (Routledge, 1996)

Hewer S, *Text Manipulation – computer-based activities to improve knowledge and use of the target language,* InfoTech 2 (CILT, 1997)

Holmes B, 'Differentiation in the foreign classroom', in Swarbrick, A (ed) *Teaching Modern Languages* (OU, 1994)

Little D, *Learner autonomy 1: definitions, issues and problems* (Authentik, 1989)

Page B, *Letting go, taking hold – a guide to independent language learning by teachers for teachers* (CILT, 1992)

Parr H, *Assessment and planning in the MFL department,* Pathfinder 29 (CILT, 1997)

Waterhouse P, *Flexible learning: an outline (*Network Educational Press, 1990)

Wringe C, *The Effective Teaching of Modern Languages* (Longman, 1989)

c*i*LT